AF894255

YOUR DREAM IS MY DREAM

How My Personal Immigration Story
Can Help You Achieve The American Dream™

Ahmad Yakzan, Esq.

Copyright © 2021 by American Dream™ Law Office

All rights reserved. No part of this publication may be reproduced, distributed, or transmitted in any form or by any means, including photocopying, recording, or other electronic or mechanical methods, without the prior written permission of the publisher, except in the case of brief quotations embodied in critical reviews and certain other noncommercial uses permitted by copyright law. For permission requests, write to the publisher, addressed "Attention: Permissions Coordinator," at the address below.

Jacobs & Whitehall
73-03 Bell Blvd, #10
Oakland Gardens, NY 11364
(888) 570-7338
www.jacobsandwhitehall.com

Ordering Information:

Quantity sales. Special discounts are available on quantity purchases by corporations, associations, and others. For details, contact the publisher at the address above.

Orders by U.S. trade bookstores and wholesalers. Please contact Jacobs & Whitehall: Tel: (888) 991-2766 or visit www.jacobsandwhitehall.com.

Printed in the United States of America

Published in 2021

ISBN: 978-1-954506-14-5

PREFACE

Many authors have written about immigration; I wrote this book from my perspective as an immigrant, who, like many others came to the United States in pursuit of the American Dream™. I write this book to let you know that Your American Dream™ is possible. I write from your perspective because I have been in your shoes. I came to the United States at a young age, got the best education I could get, and became a citizen of this great country. I know you can reach the same goal with the right help.

I did not reach my dream without people's help. Numerous people in the United States helped me reach my goal. To the faculty, staff of and trustees of Stetson University, thank you for believing in me when it was hard for me to believe in myself.

To James Thaler, Mike Gordon, and their families, thank you for being the family I needed when I felt alone in this world.

To my clients and staff, thank you for always making me a better attorney.

To everyone who reads this book, I know your American Dream™ is possible. I share that dream with you. Your dream is exactly mine. I hope this book helps you get closer to yours.

DEDICATION

This book is dedicated to my mother, whose patience and prayers led me to my American Dream™.

Ahmad Yakzan

Disclaimer

This publication is intended to be used for educational purposes only. No legal advice is being given, and no attorney-client relationship is intended to be created by reading this material. The author assumes no liability for any errors or omissions or for how this book or its contents are used or interpreted, or for any consequences resulting directly or indirectly from the use of this book. For legal or any other advice, please consult an experienced attorney or the appropriate expert, who is aware of the specific facts of your case and is knowledgeable in the law in your jurisdiction. No statement should be construed as a promise of a particular result in any case.

American Dream™ Law Office PLLC
4451 Park Blvd. N.
Pinellas Park, FL 33781
(888)963 7326
www.americandreamlawoffice.com

TESTIMONIALS

"Mr. Ahmad Yakzan provided a level of expert professional service that was exceptional in every way. I was on the other side of the world, which presented an additional layer of challenges in terms of processing my spouse's visa. Mr. Yakzan was always able to find times between time zones to speak when needed. While the process is time-consuming, it would have been overwhelming without the expertise of Mr. Yakzan."

– Greg

****

"My dad has been in the immigration for more than 29 years and every lawyer we spoke to before Ahmad told him not to mess with his case. Ahmad was able to find out they were all wrong. He reopened my dad's case and today my father became a permanent resident. I highly recommend this amazing lawyer!!"

– A Satisfied Client

****

"I hired Mr. Yakzan to assist us with obtaining a green card for my spouse, who is from the UK. He was extremely knowledgeable about the process and answered all of our questions thoroughly. His costs were reasonable, and we ended up getting everything done much faster than we had anticipated!"

– Jaimee C.

****

"My fiancé and I recently met with Mr. Yakzan to discuss our immigration case that involves a removal order. Mr. Yakzan was extremely informative and genuinely interested in keeping our family together (we also have a young daughter). Although we are not able to pursue a resolution to our case at this time because of financial reasons, we look forward to working with him in the future."

– Tara

****

"Every single step of my journey, from leaving my home country to me being allowed to stay here in the U.S, has gone exactly as Mr. Yakzan said it would. He advised and guided me every step of the way, and thanks to his highly professional help, I am able to have a life here, with my wife and child. I would highly recommend Mr. Yakzan to anyone considering moving to the U.S."

– Michael H.

****

Table Of Contents

About The Author

I was born in Saudi Arabia; my parents were Lebanese. In 1986, in the middle of a civil war in Lebanon, we moved from Saudi Arabia to Lebanon because my Dad wanted us to learn English because the educational system was much better. I grew up in a war-torn country. My elementary school was literally in the middle of the warring factions, so when they started shooting rockets at each other, we were right in the middle. That war ended in 1992, and I went to High School in Lebanon and the day I was graduating from High School, I got my papers to come here to the United States which was a big thing. I had uncles leave but not just children. So, I remember my mother just hugging me in the middle of a basketball court and just started crying. The problem was she was probably right because she didn't get to see me for 17 years.

So, I had just turned 18, packed my things, and a month later, I'm in the United States on my own. I've had to stay in the United States and my mother didn't want me to come back until I got my permanent residence and that whole story took about 17 years. I've always wanted to go to law school since I was 15 and when I was at community college and an alumni told me why don't you think of going to Stetson? I'm like Oh awesome! Stetson. She told me a little bit about Stetson and I started here and I sent a request to the Law School because, in Lebanon, the law is an undergraduate thing, you don't have to get an undergraduate degree before going to law school. So, they said, you need to speak to DeLand because that's where our main campus is, you need to get your bachelor's. So, I ended up having to pay the same amount of money if I had gone there or UCF, which I was like accepted on the spot because they had some kind of deal with the community college where I was and I ended up at Stetson.

I thank God every day that I ended up there. It was amazing. In 2001, I was the only Arabic, Muslim international student at Stetson on an F-1 visa, I think Stetson had 110 international students and after 9/11, it just dropped. It wasn't only Arabs but I was the only one who was a Muslim on 9/11 who was a part of "special registration". Special registration was pretty much every person on a visa from any Muslim country needs to come in and do and register with the United States federal government. My international student advisor at the time, Tracy Partin took me down to Orlando where I had to get registered. It had a different feel to it, I mean, I became an orientation leader, I don't know if it's still called the same thing or not. They really calmed me down at Stetson. I had faced a lot of discrimination at community college and I mean, it really opened my eyes, what I had to face there.

Let me tell you, in community college, I'd been in the US for 2 months and my psychology professor asked me if I had a bomb in my backpack. That did not happen at Stetson. If I had ever faced anything, which I didn't, it probably would not have been from the faculty, it would have been from the students. When 9/11 happened, the head of the Political Science Department, where I was a student and an assistant, came to me and said, if anybody opens their mouth about you and mind you, I was the only international Muslim student, we are going to kick them out of school. So, Stetson was family, Stetson is still family. Stetson made me meet a lot of lifelong friends that I can never live without and that's how Stetson was and how Stetson still is. Dr. T. Wayne Bailey, I know he doesn't like to admit it, but he is, and I said it at his retirement party that my American Dream™ would not have been possible without him because even when I was ready to give up he did not give up on me; I didn't do well on the LSAT or when I didn't get a job or something like that, he was always there even though he made me hear a couple of times but that man moved mountains for me to be where I am today.

I don't want to exclude anyone, because he is just one of many. They just really taught me the meaning of philanthropy and how you need to help people for you to succeed and this is exactly what they did for 11 years that I was at Stetson. After undergrad, I got a job in

Volusia County, Matt was the Assistant County Manager at Volusia County and Dr. Bailey spoke to him and I got an internship with them and then, I was gearing up to go to Law School and that did not come through, the funding was a little stalled. So, they told me, why don't you come and get an MBA in the meantime.

Dr. Frank Dezort was the head of the program. He spoke to the Dean and said we have one or two scholarships, I know one is taken, the other scholarship I want to go to Ahmad and at the time, I didn't even think I would go to Business School. I'm terrible at numbers. I did my MBA for a full year and then maybe a week before having to start law school, the other money came in for that because I had half for the law school at that point and then the other half came 3 or 4 days before the law school and I was actually in the middle of a recession, I couldn't find a job. So, I got the money for Law School and 2006 is when I moved to St Pete. I remember in December 15th , 2005, that was my graduation from MBA and I was in a chapel, every single dean was there including President Lee and we were all in awe.

I was walking around not believing that I would go to law school. It's a dream that I had for about 10 years at that point. I had moved to the United States from the Middle East. just for it to happen and for it to finally actually just happen, I was in awe. I was in a trance the whole MBA graduation. I was the last one and everybody on the stage hugged me and they were just very excited for me and I really don't know how to describe it. It's just that I go back to thinking about that night and Dr. Ballinger was there and he always told me I'm always going to be on your team. I could not believe that it's happening. I just couldn't. I don't know how to describe it, I really don't.

I was very proud to graduate but getting to be an attorney wasn't easy. I mean I couldn't work the first year of Law School and I was living on $200 a month. My dorm was paid for, my phone was paid for because we had phones in the dorm but I was literally living on $200 a month and I made it. I don't know, how.

I did it because I wanted to do Human Rights Advocacy for Muslim women and I do a lot of that work now. But I went to DC, after graduating, and got a job and they were going to pay me $38,000 in DC, which wouldn't even pay for rent there. Professor Dorthea Bean, she was one of my Human Rights professors, sat me down and said, "you need to learn how to become an attorney and that work will come through". Art Rios, one of my mentors, sat me down and said you need to go into immigration because you make friends very quickly. I started working for free for someone for 6 months and she applied for my H-1B visa after I graduated from law school.

Then, I passed the Bar, after a struggle. The other law clerk she had actually become an attorney left. So, I became an attorney and then went to a different law firm and petitioned for my green card and in 2015, I got it because of the work I did at Stetson University and at the Law School, helped me become the best attorney I could be. I lucked out when I got my work visa in 2010. The visas were not running up because we had a bad economy. I then transferred to another law firm and that law firm actually applied for my green card.

It took about a year and a half to do because they had to prove that no one in my vicinity could actually do my job and I do a lot of that work now but they had to prove that they are not displacing another American worker. So, they petitioned and once I got the green card, I had a dispute with them over compensation and I was let go the day I was going to Lebanon after 17 years.

My family has grown a lot in the prior 17 or 18 years since I left. It was tough, it really was. I mean I missed everything back home from everybody getting married to my sister growing up and graduating from college, to my parents getting divorced. I was the only Ahmad in the family when I left, now there are 6 or 7. All these cousins I didn't even know.

The bottom line is, anybody there would have traded places with me; they would have been very happy to do so. They would have taken this opportunity and came to the United States and done what I have done without hesitation.

Yeah, it was tough; it was hard but in the end, I made it. Coming to America was a big thing. I mean it's still the big thing, it's still the American Dream™, it's still a success, it's still if you work hard, you are going to make it and that's the whole idea of the American Dream™. I've met so many people in Stetson University and outside of Stetson who have worked very hard to reach their American Dream™. This is the land of dreams. Lady Liberty is not just in my logo. We practice what she signifies every day at the American Dream™ Law Office. We remember new immigrants gazing with awe at her face every time we meet a new client pursuing his or her American Dream™. Seeing that twinkle in a client's eyes when she becomes a citizen or receives her permanent residence is worth millions of dollars.

Why Did You Want To Write This Book?

I want people to believe that their American Dream™ is possible. Over the last four years, a lot of my clients have started to believe that the American Dream™ isn't possible anymore because of US policies, and they stopped wanting to try. A lot of people say that the American Dream™ is dead, but I don't think it will ever be dead. If I can show someone how to get there, why shouldn't I?

In addition to wanting to explain to people that it's still doable, I want people to know that I understand what they're going through because I've gone through it myself. I went through the process of obtaining my visa in Lebanon and getting an education, work visa, and green card until finally, I gained citizenship. I know what it means to my clients and I know how they are going to feel once they get through all of the steps. What better advocate can a person ask for?

Chapter 1

What Was Your Life Like Before Coming To The United States?

I'm Ahmad Yakzan, and I'm originally from Lebanon. I got my citizenship since then, but I've been an immigrant all of my life. I was born in Saudi Arabia to Lebanese parents, and when I was about six years old, my dad wanted us to get a better education, so he sent us to Lebanon. Between the ages of 6 and 12, I lived through that Lebanese Civil War, which was ongoing from 1975 until about 1992. It wasn't until 1998 that I left the country.

I had a rough childhood. Not only did I move around a lot, but my school was between the Christian and the Muslim part of Beirut. Usually, a window seat for the view would have been in high demand, but in my school, it was the opposite, since the glass would shatter with each bomb that was dropped. Since age 15, it was my dream to move to the United States and become an attorney. My desire to become an attorney was sparked when a friend of mine, who was part of one of the first recycling clubs in Lebanon, told me I would make a great international attorney, which would not only allow me to make money but help people. I started asking myself, why not become an attorney?

Fortunately, my dad had a friend who lived in the US and helped me apply to colleges while I was still in Lebanon. At age 17, on the day of my high school graduation, I received my acceptance letter and Form I-20, which made me eligible for nonimmigrant student status. I remember that day as if it was yesterday. After most people had left, my mom handed me the packet with those documents, hugged me in the middle of the basketball court, and just started crying. Everyone said, "You need to stop crying so your son won't start crying."

After that, I took a vacation for about five months while waiting for everything to go through. At the time, Lebanon didn't have a consulate, so we had to go to Damascus to get the visa. The first time I went, I wasn't 18 years old, so they told me I needed to come back with my parents, and they scheduled me to do so on October 5th, 1998. When I finally got the visa, I was screaming at the top of my lungs. Having prayed for this day, my grandma began crying and just hugged me. A month later, I was in the US. In retrospect, I wish I hadn't moved so quickly, because I didn't get to see my family for over 17 years. I wish I'd had more time with them.

What Does The American Dream™ Mean To You?

Everyone has their own idea of the American Dream™, so I never try to define it for them; one person's American Dream™ might be to run a clinic, and another person's American Dream™ might be to run a landscaping company. My American Dream™ is to be the best immigration attorney I possibly can be and to run a successful practice in order to help people, and not worry about living paycheck to paycheck.

Being financially secure is probably one of the most sought-after aspects of the American Dream™ since many of us have come to the United States from war-torn countries. Having the ability to own your own home is another common part of the American Dream™. After renting for a long time, I finally bought my first house last year. Another aspect of the American Dream™ is security in the sense of safety. When I was in Lebanon, I had to worry about being killed by a stray bullet or a bomb, and while I know that happens in the US too, it doesn't happen as often.

I do not think there is one definition for "the American Dream™," because the meaning of it can evolve. When I came to the US, my dream was to become an attorney, and then it was to get my work visa and green card, after which it became running my own firm, and with the help of Speakeasy, expanding my firm. Now, my dream is to keep my house and have a family. The American Dream™ can mean many different things to different people, but it almost always means security.

Did Your Experience As An Immigrant Play Into The Direction Of Your Career?

I never thought that I would practice immigration law; in fact, I resisted the idea for a very long time. I wanted to become an international human rights lawyer at the United Nations, but even the entry-level position at the United Nations is very hard to get, so I interviewed with several NGOs in Washington DC. However, they wanted to pay me only $38,000. That was in 2009, and it dawned on me that I didn't have a job and didn't know what I was going to do after graduating from law school. That's when one of my mentors sat me down and said, "You need to practice immigration law," to which I responded, "Why would I want to do that?" He said, "Because you make friends very easily, and that's half of being an immigration attorney."

After that, another mentor in law school gave me the phone number for someone who needed an Arabic speaker, and I ended up working for that person for six months. It was an internship, and then I got hired as a law clerk. When I passed the bar, I took over the other attorney's job because he had left. I suppose the circumstances led me to immigration law, and when I started practicing it, I absolutely loved it. I could be making a lot more money doing something else, but I don't do it just for the money; the sparkle in a client's eye who just got their green card or citizenship is worth millions. I know what it's like because I just recently went through my own citizenship interview (funny enough, the officers thought I was representing my attorney, not the other way around).

CHAPTER 2

MOST PRESSING ISSUES FACED BY IMMIGRANTS TO THE US CURRENTLY

I believe that the US system lacks a long-term vision. I recently spoke to someone who received a master's degree in information technology in the US. He is going to have to return to India because there are no visa numbers available for him to stay here. When people hear the term 'immigration,' unfortunately, they usually think of illegal immigration; they don't think about the fact that immigrants are actually needed in order to keep the American Dream™ alive—we need people who are doctors, IT professionals, etc.

The system in the United States is reactive rather than proactive. If immigration reform happens, it's because we want to help 13 or 16 million people here. We want to support DACA because we're getting political pressure. In most other countries, at least in the developing world, they know what they need. For example, in Canada, Australia, and Europe, they know how many professionals of a certain type they will need in a given year. One of my cousins is an engineer and the other is a nurse, and they just went to Germany because Germany needs engineers and nurses.

The US lacks a long-term vision for attracting the people it needs. Currently, there are so many DACA recipients who work in the healthcare field, and instead of offering them status, we try to take it away from them. In contrast, France just gave automatic citizenship to every single immigrant who's working to fight COVID-19; imagine if the US were to do that.

The biggest impediment is the system, and unfortunately, a lot of immigrants believe that they can navigate it by themselves. However, it is a complicated system, and not having an attorney is a detriment. A former Assistant Director of the Department of Homeland Security said that immigration law is very complex, and the person who knows how to navigate it is worth their weight in gold. This is something I believe, and it's why people need to hire someone who understands the system (which is something that even some immigration lawyers have trouble with).

If we were to simplify the system and base it on what type of immigrants we want, immigrants would have an easier time navigating it. The immigration court system is very complex, and we need a vision in the United States of attracting the people who we really need for building a future. One of the founders of Google or LinkedIn was on an H-1B visa or an L-1 visa and almost lost it; this is a person who spent millions of dollars on his work, and we were going to kick him out. I think the biggest obstacle to immigrants is actually the system itself.

What Challenges Have You And Others Faced While Immigrating To The United States?

Three of the main challenges faced by people who are trying to immigrate to the United States are the complexity of the system, knowing which visa can be obtained and how, and money. Immigration attorneys are not cheap, especially for someone who is in a removal proceeding. Ultimately, the challenges will depend on the individual's circumstances. What it comes down to is figuring out how to reach the goal, but some goals are attainable and some aren't.

In addition to being complex, the system favors people who have money. For example, if someone spends half a million dollars or a million dollars in the United States, then they will get a green card right away. However, for someone who is poor, it will take a very long time to get a green card, especially if they're from Mexico, the Philippines, Vietnam, or India. It becomes important to have a map for getting to one's destination, although that can be hard, especially since the system is full of impediments.

CHAPTER 3

CURRENT STATUS OF DACA AND EXPECTED CHANGES UNDER THE BIDEN ADMINISTRATION

DACA is currently in a state of flux, due to the Supreme Court ruling that Trump had the power to take it away but that he didn't follow the Administrative Procedures Act, which applicants had relied on for years, in doing so. By ruling that it is within President Trump's power to take the program away, the Supreme Court also tacitly ruled that President Obama did actually have the power to enact the DACA program in the first place. This helps DACA recipients by giving them the argument that DACA is a legal program. USCIS responded by saying they were not going to abide by the Supreme Court ruling because it was not final (due to the Supreme Court sending it back to the lower court), even though they technically should be following the ruling.

President Biden's administration has signed an executive order to extend DACA. I've added links about this and other potential immigration reforms on my website, which you can view by going to 2021immigrationreform.com.

How Has COVID-19 Impacted The DACA Recipients?

DACA recipients have been impacted in two major ways. The first is that thousands of DACA recipients are working on the frontlines of the pandemic as doctors and nurses. Many doctors are here on DACA or J visas. In September, USCIS announced they would close a lot of their offices due to financial strain during the pandemic. That means that the processing times have been significantly prolonged, which is the second major impact of COVID on DACA recipients. While the delay in processing affects every immigrant, it especially affects DACA recipients because they can lose their work permits.

What Do The Wolf Memo And The Edlow Memo Say?

The Wolf memo and the Edlow memo both deal with DACA. In addition to saying the administration is not going to accept any new DACA applications, the memos also limited approvals for DACA applications from two years, per President Obama's original DACA order, to one year. These memos essentially limited who can apply under the program after it was taken away by the administration two years ago.

The Trump administration wrote these memos while losing their case at the Supreme Court, which ruled that the government actually put away DACA in violation of the due process rights of the petitioners (the organizations that sued on behalf of the people). Specifically, the Supreme Court said that the government did have the right to end DACA but, in doing so, had violated the procedures under the Administrative Procedures Act (APA).

As an interesting aside, a New York judge ruled this month that U.S. Department of Homeland Security (DHS) Acting Secretary Chad Wolf was not appointed to be the head of USCIS in the proper way. Under the Federal Succession Act, memos signed by someone in an acting capacity at DHS are actually illegal. That means no one has to follow the Wolf Memo.

In the few months that President Biden has been in office, he has signed several executive orders to protect DACA recipients. He has also changed prosecutorial discretion rules to protect parents of United States citizens who would have qualified for DAPA. He has also introduced a very progressive immigration law that would help both populations. I hope that Congress passes this new law that would protect millions of people from deportation.

CHAPTER 4

CAN I FILE FOR A RENEWAL OF DACA IF IT EXPIRES SOON?

If your DACA expires soon or if it has already been expired, go ahead and apply for renewal; at the very least, that will put you in the queue to apply for permanent residence should the law be extended for people who were DACA recipients as of a certain date. Being in the queue also means that if you get denied illegally, you can actually sue the federal government to get DACA, which is how many of those lawsuits began.

On a Facebook group for federal litigation, the advice that all immigration attorneys are giving is to go ahead and apply, and if you get denied, we'll go through the federal court if we need to. With thousands of people following that advice, a lawsuit could become a class action, which would be major litigation against the government.

What If I Never Had DACA? Can I Apply Now?

If you never had DACA, I recommend you apply anyways. The program is probably going to be extended soon, leading to an influx of applicants, and when that happens, you'll have priority if you applied before the 21st of January. Even though USCIS is currently rejecting first-time applicants (in spite of the Supreme Court ruling), a New York judge has ordered them to begin accepting them. Impending changes could pave the way for new applicants.

I Trusted the Government With My Data When I Applied for DACA. Can They Use That Information to Deport Me?

Under the actual DACA program, there is a promise that the government will not use information you've provided in any way to get you deported. Over the last four years, however, there was still fear that the administration might use the information to deport immigrants anyways. If that were to happen, you should hire a good immigration attorney to defend you, and you could actually sue under the Federal Administrative Procedures Act. Federal law should protect you since DACA was an executive order.

CHAPTER 5

DEFERRED ACTION FOR PARENTS OF AMERICANS AND LAWFUL PERMANENT RESIDENTS PROGRAM

DAPA is the same as DACA but for people who are parents of United States Citizens and permanent residents. It's estimated that there are about 13 million undocumented immigrants who have children or a spouse who are United States citizens. DAPA is intended to stop people with immediate relatives who are citizens or permanent residents from being deported if they themselves don't qualify under DACA.

What Were the Proposed DAPA Eligibility Requirements?

The DAPA requirements are very close to those of the DACA program. You have to be the parent of a United States citizen or permanent resident. You must have lived in the United States since January 1st, 2010, the date of the DAPA order (which is different from the DACA date, as DAPA was an extension of the second DACA order), and you must have been present in the US on January 1st, 2010. You should not have had legal status at the time that the order was actually executed.

Additionally, you cannot have been convicted of a criminal offense, including both felonies and grave misdemeanors. Because the Immigration and Nationality Act (INA) doesn't specify what should be considered a serious misdemeanor, it's up to USCIS to determine, and there has been a lot of debate over what should and should not be considered. The current definition from USCIS is either a crime involving moral turpitude (CIMT) or an aggravated felony resulting in more than one year in jail. In 2010, possession was causing many applications to be rejected, so this definition attempts to address offenses for weed or similar convictions (which can be waived with a waiver).

Where Does Comprehensive Immigration Reform Stand At The End Of 2020?

Immigration reform is currently halted, pending the results of the two special elections in Georgia and the Biden immigration plan. When the Georgia Democrats take their two seats, they will have the majority in the Senate (with Kamala Harris acting as a tie-breaker), meaning it will be easier for President Biden to pass immigration laws. The problem with immigration reform before was that something might pass in the Senate but not in the House because one party had control. Now, there will be unified control for the first year of Biden's administration.

What Are the Issues With the DREAM Act?

The problem with DACA is that it's an executive order. It wasn't established by law, so any subsequent president can come in and nullify it, as President Trump tried to do with President Obama's DACA order, and take the program away from all of the people who applied for it. The DREAM Act is supposed to codify DACA (put it in the law) and give the Dreamers a path to citizenship.

One major issue they've had for a long time as they've tried to pass the DREAM Act is the question of whether we're going to allow Dreamers that path to citizenship or not. Not giving them citizenship might not actually be legal. The alternative would be to let them have green cards forever. Republicans want to give Dreamers green cards instead of letting them naturalize because they think that the Dreamers will probably lean more toward the Democratic Party. If Dreamers become citizens, they could theoretically file for their parents, which could add even more Democrat voters and threaten the Republican Party's ability to win elections. Democrats, on the other hand, want Dreamers to be able to obtain their citizenship and petition for their parents.

The Democratic Party's failure to pass the DREAM Act in 2012 has presented a problem for them ever since. With unified control in 2021, the Dream Act could finally be passed.

CHAPTER 6

WHAT IS DEFERRED ACTION IMMIGRATION?

Deferred action under the Immigration and Naturalization Act is an executive power that the president has to stop the deportation or to defer the removal, of a person or a group of people that the president believes are not actually supposed to be let go. The Temporary Protected Status (TPS) is another sort of deferred action where they don't enforce a removal if you've personally been involved in a problem or if your country had an issue. Haitians were given TPS after the

2010 earthquake, though Trump has tried to take it away, and Liberians have had it since 1992. Cubans have also been getting paroled since the 1950s, though that was stopped under President Trump.

On a side note, another popular program that was taken away by the Trump administration is the one for spouses of service members. If you were married to someone in the Armed Forces, they would give you advanced parole into the United States, even if you were out of status. After that, you were eligible for a green card.

On What Grounds Is Deferred Action Immigration Granted?

The answer depends on which program we are talking about. When President Obama tried to extend DACA and establish DAPA, some people said he didn't have the power to do so. I believe that under the law he actually has the power to defer whomever he wants. There should not be limitations.

How Do I Apply for Deferred Action in My Immigration Case?

The application process depends on the program. For most of them, you need to apply through USCIS with a form. For example, the DACA program invented a new form G-325A for biographic information, and it also has a special form for DACA recipients, the petition for deferred action itself, plus the I-212 for reapplying after removal or deportation. If you are in immigration court and you get deferred action with a service, the judge can either terminate the case or administratively close it.

CHAPTER 7

WHY IS IT IMPORTANT TO FIND AN IMMIGRATION ATTORNEY?

A friend of mine asked me why I don't practice more than one type of law, and after thinking about it for a minute, I responded by saying that I just want my focus to be 100 percent on immigration. If I were to add more practice areas, I would probably hire another attorney rather than do it myself. This is not to say that an attorney who practices more than one type of law is not necessarily a good immigration attorney, but some attorneys think that immigration is just about filling out forms, which is not true.

There is a saying between attorneys that an attorney who practices everything is good at nothing. I don't believe that an attorney who handles all types of cases is going to be a good immigration attorney, because immigration law is very complex. An attorney who specializes in immigration law is going to know more about it than someone who practices in other areas of the law, and will always keep ahead of the latest developments in immigration law.

For example, I've been calling my clients who are DACA recipients to let them know that they should expect something to change in January, and I highly doubt that someone who doesn't practice immigration exclusively would know that. Hiring someone who practices immigration law exclusively is the best course of action because they're going to know exactly what are their clients' needs, when they'll need it, and how to guide them through the system. An attorney who specializes in immigration law will only know the immigration system, which is a good thing because attorneys who work within too many systems can get them bungled up in their head.

What Specific Areas of Immigration Law Does Your Firm Handle?

I handle every aspect of immigration law. I have completed almost every single petition available, and about 75 percent of them have been through federal litigation and immigration court.

CHAPTER 8

WHAT KIND OF CLIENTS DO YOU ASSIST?

I've represented people from all over the world except the penguins in Antarctica. My clients don't fall under one profile. I represent people who are trying to extend a visa, as well as people who are trying to spend a million dollars in the US in order to get a green card. A common thread among all of my clients is the desire to achieve the American Dream™. I have even represented people who've been in the US since before I was born. In fact, during my first legal job, one of my first clients had a green card that was literally green (they are no longer green); he had received it on Ellis Island in the 1950s. I represent investors overseas and investors in the US who need to apply for a change of status. I represent everyone who needs immigration help.

What Are Some Of The Common Struggles That People Have When It Comes To Finding Immigration Legal Services Here In The US?

Many lawyers are money hungry and will charge a lot but will fail to deliver on their promises. Other lawyers will charge a very small amount, but as a result, they will have to rush their clients through the system in order to not lose money. When it comes to costs, I put myself in the middle. I'm going to tell clients the truth from the beginning, and if I charge a little more than some other attorneys, it's because I give each and every case the personal attention it deserves.

I will explain to a client why they might not win their case, and tell them what I can do for them. In contrast, a lot of lawyers will sign up clients without telling them the truth and set expectations that can't be met. When clients lose under these circumstances, it becomes easy for them to assume that all lawyers are the same.

Unfortunately, the attorneys who just fill out forms often end up creating big problems for their clients, including putting them in removal proceedings. Bar associations around the country know that simply filling out the forms is not equivalent to practicing law, but the USCIS says it is. As a result, people overseas often harbor a lot of distrust. Many of these people will assume that I am going to take their money and do nothing for them, often because that's exactly what other attorneys before me chose to do.

Distrust in immigration practitioners is very high. A lawyer might have 500 5-star reviews, but if they don't do what they promise, then those reviews don't matter. I tell people to not only look at the reviews but actually call the firm and see how the intake person treats them.

Honestly, immigration law is very consuming and very draining. I have a client right now who's been in detention for eight months, despite having gotten into a stay of removal. If a phone call comes in at 11 o'clock at night, it has to be answered, because that might be the last time to communicate with a client before they go into court.

CHAPTER 9

WHAT MAKES IMMIGRANTS VULNERABLE TO BAD ATTORNEYS OR SERVICES?

If an immigrant is working without authorization and making money under the table, and one service promises to help them for $500, while an experienced immigration attorney promises to help them for $5,000, which will the person likely choose? Of course, they're going to choose the non-attorney service for $500, and that's the issue.

On two occasions, I had to intervene in a conversation that was taking place in the Miami Asylum Office in Florida, where people become translators. The first time, there was a non-attorney giving legal advice in Arabic right in front of me. I happened to be on the elevator with the officer right afterward, and I said, "That guy was just giving legal advice; what are you going to do about it?" He responded with, "I'm not going to do anything. I'm probably going to deny the case anyways, so why even bother?"

On the second occasion, what I heard was egregious. I was sitting in the waiting area, where a Muslim dad (alongside his son) was praying for his wife who was being interviewed to be allowed inside. Then, a "translator" came out and said, "Did you like how I changed the answers to those questions? We are lucky that the translator on the phone didn't actually pick up on that." As an attorney, I have an ethical duty to report something like that, so I did. I told the manager that the person was very loudly proclaiming that he changed the answers and that while I didn't want to mess with the family's future, I had to say something. After that, they called him back, and I don't know what happened. I met with the fraud detection unit afterward to explain what happened.

On top of there already being a lot of distrust in lawyers, there are people who are pretending to be lawyers. I've reported someone to the Florida Bar for doing something which led my client to end up in removal proceedings, and the attitude was that they're not doing it anymore. The person ended up being prosecuted in federal court in the Middle District of Florida because he was embezzling money from his client. The Florida Bar said they're not doing it anymore, and asked what they should do about it. That is the attitude here, and that has bred a lot of distrust in immigration attorneys.

Another challenge is that many people don't know what they qualify for. I had a client who had been here for a long time, but her DACA application was denied. She didn't know that she qualified for a green card. A lot of immigrants don't know what they qualify for, and unfortunately, they fall for false promises. Finding a good immigration attorney is a struggle, and a lot of websites are just hyped up. If someone doesn't feel comfortable around an attorney, then they shouldn't hire them, because the client and attorney need to click.

CHAPTER 10

CONSEQUENCES IMMIGRANTS FACE FROM HIRING AN INEXPERIENCED ATTORNEY

If an immigrant hires an inadequate attorney or non-attorney service to handle their case, they could end up being denied, or even find themselves in removal proceedings. As a result, they will end up paying significantly more money than they would have had they hired the right attorney from the beginning.

I once represented a husband and wife, and the wife (who was from China) had previously hired a

Chinese attorney to handle her asylum case. This attorney made up a story for her. If a client were to ask me to do that for them, I would kick them out of my office. If it doesn't look like a couple is truly married, then I will kick them out of my office. The Chinese attorney's story didn't add up, and he included the fact that she had been married to two different people in China prior to coming to the United States.

I was hired to accompany this couple to a green card interview. During that interview, the officer brought up the fact that in the previous case, the wife stated that she had been married twice before. In response, the wife said that she had only been married once. The previous lawyer who had helped with the asylum application misspelled her former husband's name. Furthermore, she wasn't able to get a divorce certificate for two different people from China, because under oath she said she'd been married twice before. However, this was a mistake made by the translator. This is an example of a client who had a bona fide case, yet was denied due to an error made by the translator. Immigration law can be done in a bad way, which can cause major consequences for the client.

If An Immigrant's Case Is Mishandled By A Non-Attorney Service, Will That Hurt Their Chances Of A Successful Immigration Case In The Future?

It may be hard to believe, but as the law stands right now, an immigrant who knowingly hires a non-attorney service that provides poor advice and causes the case to be denied could get deported. In immigration law, a person doesn't have to be an attorney to appear in immigration court. There are wonderful representatives who work for Catholic Charities who advocate on behalf of clients, and while they are accredited representatives and good people, they are not lawyers. The level of work that a client will get from an attorney is different, but some people can't afford it, which is understandable.

One of my clients who is currently in detention hired a non-lawyer prior to hiring me. That non-lawyer can no longer appear in court because he lost his accreditation. That non-lawyer was working with a criminal attorney who showed up to the individual hearing, which is the merits hearing in immigration court. The whole transcript of the individual hearing was 40 pages, and I've had 300 to 500-page transcripts.

On top of that, it was the first or second time that the attorney had ever met the client in person, and he didn't know that the client was actually eligible for asylum. The first thing that he said at the merits hearing was, "Your Honor, I just spoke to my client's brother and he qualifies for asylum." Of course, he hadn't submitted an application, so he couldn't prove that he actually had an asylum case.

Once I was hired by this client, I had to explain to him that he was going to be screwed if we didn't go after the attorney. After a lot of convincing, he agreed. I hate going after other attorneys. I never put my name on a bar complaint because I know what that means. I've had it done to me for personal reasons, and it's absolutely gut-wrenching to be in front of the bar responding to a complaint, but some attorneys deserve it.

What Qualifications Should Someone Be Looking For In An Immigration Attorney?

An immigrant should ask prospective immigration attorneys three questions: whether or not they have practiced immigration law exclusively, whether or not they are an immigrant themselves and have lived the experience, and whether or not they have handled a case that is similar to theirs. Attorneys can't guarantee a result, so they have to be transparent with clients by letting them know that just because a similar case had a certain outcome doesn't mean that will necessarily be the outcome in their case.

The immigrant should also ask the attorney about their outlook, and try to determine whether they find the attorney to be trustworthy. If it doesn't seem like the attorney is telling the truth, then they shouldn't be hired. If someone's gut is telling them not to hire a particular attorney, then they should listen to their gut. Some lawyers are good people and they want clients to sign up on the spot; I want this too, but I would rather be honest with clients and tell them everything upfront before they sign because, down the road, I want their family members to hire me too.

There are times when an attorney will need to refuse a client. For example, I spoke to a woman on the phone for almost two hours and charged her nothing for it, and I also waived her consultation fee because she said that she was being abused; I believed her, and I wanted to help. However, she showed up an hour and a half late to the consultation, which took up even more of my time. At that point, I had wasted almost $2,000, and the client still wasn't respecting my time—she didn't even call to let me know that she was running late.

CHAPTER 11

HOW DO YOU HELP CLIENTS WHO FACE IMMIGRATION ISSUES?

The problem with most immigration lawyers—and I have seen this happen a million times—is that they give up the fight before it even begins, and they just admit to all of the charges in immigration court. This is akin to a defense attorney standing up in court and just saying, "I admit my client is guilty of murder." I was once a new attorney, so I know that someone who doesn't know the law is still liable for malpractice; attorneys need to educate themselves.

During immigration cases, USCIS wants attorneys to just "sit back and be quiet" (they actually told us that at a meeting in 2017). Unfortunately, a lot of attorneys actually do stay quiet and they don't fight. In addition, a lot of lawyers raise their clients' expectations too much.

If my client is in removal proceedings, I am going to fight, and if the government doesn't meet its burden, I'm going to file a motion to terminate. My approach is to be aggressive, but not too aggressive because sometimes I'll get in trouble for that. My approach is, to be honest from the beginning, and that's what I expect from my clients as well. I once fought the government for over seven years on a removal case until I won. I aim to be the biggest advocate for my client's American Dream™.

What Sets You And Your Firm Apart From The Rest?

My dream is my client's dream. A lot of immigration attorneys are either immigrant, or are married to immigrants, and there are a lot of immigration attorneys out there. I am set apart by the fact that I have not had an easy time reaching my American Dream™. I know when the American Dream™ is good for you, and when it's bad for you; I know both sides of the process. I know how it feels to fall behind or make a mistake that pushes the dream further away. I also know that the fight is worth it because I've been there; I was there when I got my green card, and I was there when the H-1B renewal process was taking longer than the government said it would. I've reached the mountain top of what I believe is my American Dream™, and I use all of my experiences to help clients reach theirs.

INDEX

NOTES